LIFT THE LID ON

MUMMIES

CONTENTS

JACQUELINE DINEEN

What are Mummies?

Mummies are the preserved bodies of the dead. When a person dies, bacteria living in water in their body causes them to rot. If their body is preserved, the rotting process is stopped. The word mummy comes from the Arabic word *mummiya,* which means bitumen, a kind of tar. When Arabs discovered the Egyptian mummies they thought they had been preserved with bitumen.

Ancient Egyptian mummies

Over five thousand years ago, the ancient Egyptian people buried their dead in shallow graves in the hot desert sand. The sand dried out the bodies leaving them perfectly preserved. The Egyptians continued to use this method to mummify their dead, until they developed a process called embalming, and preserved the bodies using chemicals and wrapping them in bandages.

The ancient Egyptians stopped burying their dead in the sand and started to bury their mummies in elaborately-decorated coffins in pyramids and tombs.

World of mummies

Mummified bodies have been found all over the world. Some have been preserved by natural methods, others artificially by using chemicals. As you read the book, use the map below to locate the places in which mummies have been discovered.

Perfect conditions

The key to preserving a body is to stop it from rotting. As well as in desert sand, mummies have been found in very cold conditions where water in the bodies has frozen solid. Mummies have also been found in the bogs of northern Europe where the lack of oxygen stops bacteria from developing and preserves the bodies.

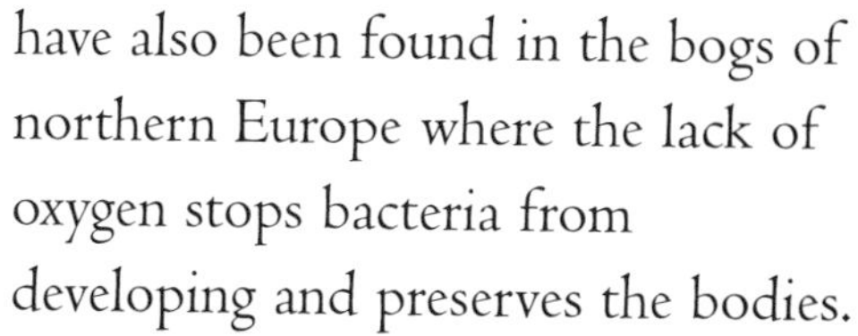

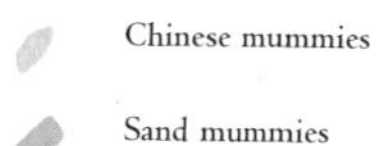

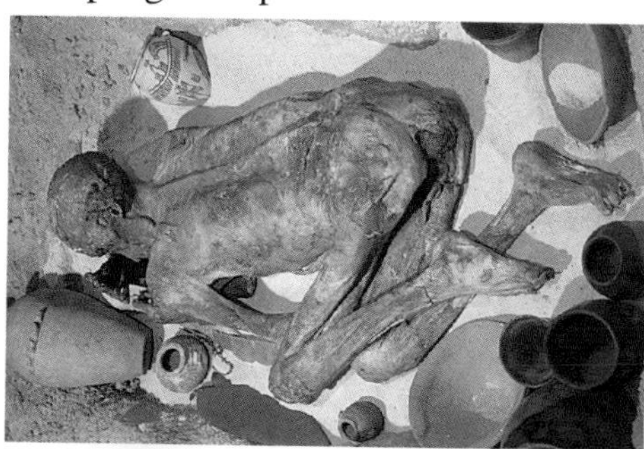

This ancient Egyptian sand mummy is known as "Ginger" because some of his red hair is still present.

Ancient Egyptian Mummies

Between 2,613 and 1,086 B.C., Egypt was one of the most advanced nations in the world. The Egyptians had strong religious beliefs. They believed that their pharaoh, the king, was a god on Earth. They also thought that if they preserved their dead, they would live forever.

The Great Pyramid is a massive 481 feet high.

Treasures of the tomb

The ancient Egyptians built huge pyramids and tombs in which to bury their dead. Often a mummy was placed in a burial chamber together with many valuable treasures, personal belongings, and household furniture. These items were to make life comfortable for the mummy during its afterlife.

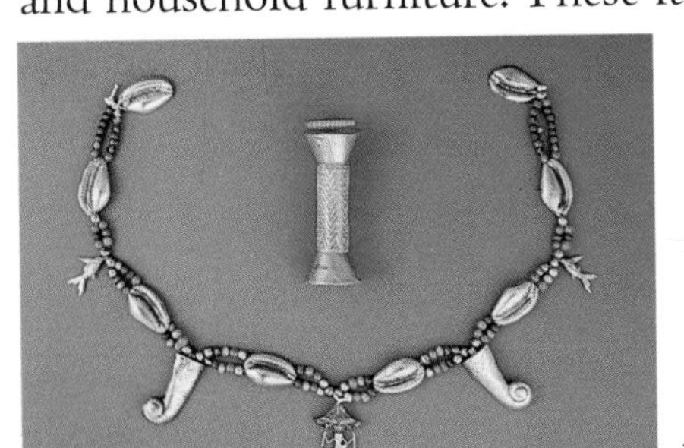

The ancient Egyptians believed their mummies would wear jewelry in the afterlife.

Long lost mummies

For thousands of years the ancient Egyptian mummies were forgotten until the French Emperor, Napoleon, invaded Egypt in 1798. In 1817 the tomb of King Seti I was found in the Valley of the Kings — a huge burial site for pharaohs. Shortly after that, forty tombs containing pharaoh mummies were discovered. Then in 1922, after a five-year search, Howard Carter discovered the 3,200 year-old tomb of the boy-pharaoh Tutankhamun.

Howard Carter

Tutankhamun's mummy was wearing a pure gold funerary mask.

Making your mummy's mask

Open the secret drawer and take out the golden funerary mask. This mask will help the gods to recognize your mummy in the afterlife. Fold back the tabs on the side of the mask and put it aside until after you have wrapped your mummy.

Rituals and Beliefs

The ancient Egyptians worshipped hundreds of gods and goddesses. Two gods, Anubis and Osiris, were important when a person died. Anubis was the god of embalming and took part in the religious ceremonies during embalming. Osiris was the god of the dead and king of the underworld. He led the mummy through the underworld, a place through which all mummies had to travel to reach the afterlife.

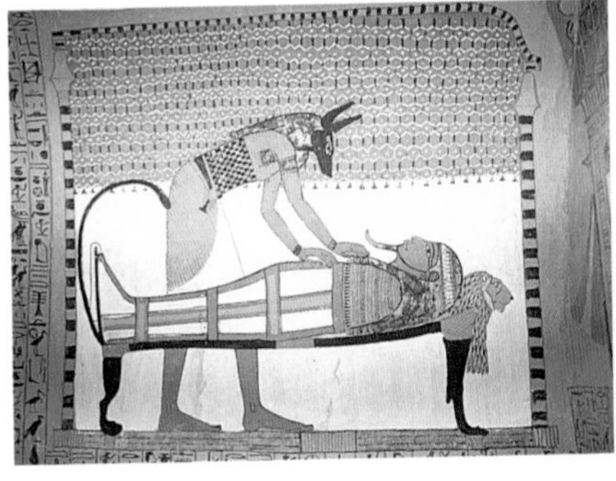

The embalmers were priests dressed as gods. The most senior priest wore the jackal-headed mask of Anubis.

Funerary beliefs

Before a mummy was buried, priests carried out sacred rituals. During one ceremony, the *Opening of the Mouth*, the priest representing the god Anubis, touched the mummy's mouth with a special tool. This let the mummy use its senses in the afterlife.

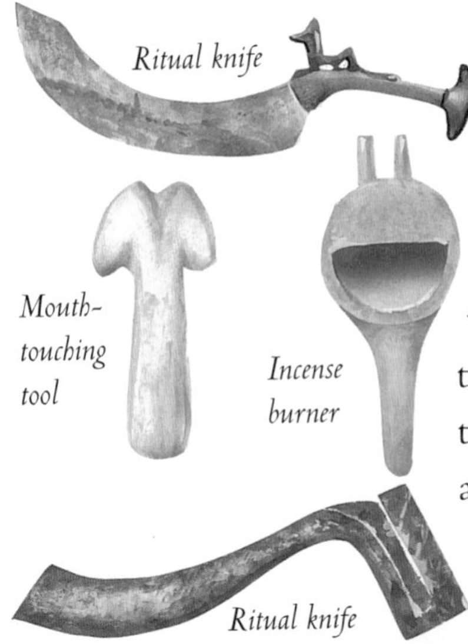

Ritual knife

Mouth-touching tool

Incense burner

Ritual knife

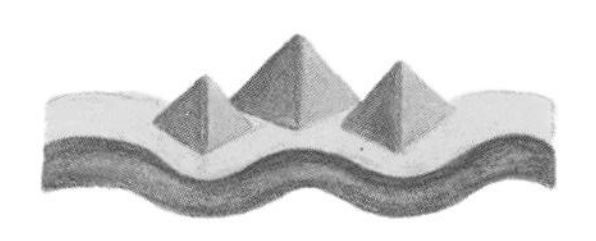

Weighing of the Heart

One of the rituals the priests acted out was the *Weighing of the Heart.*

The ancient Egyptians believed the heart, not the brain, was the center of intelligence. During the embalming process, priests placed the mummy's heart on a pair of scales and weighed it against the Feather of Truth. If the scales balanced, the mummy was believed to be truthful and sent to the afterlife. If the heart was heavier than the feather, the mummy was thought to be dishonest and as a punishment it would be devoured by the monster Ammit.

The Devourer of the Dead, Ammit, stands by ready to eat up the heart and stop the mummy from traveling into the afterlife.

Using your curse sticker

Protect your mummy by reciting the ancient "curse of the pharaoh" on the sticker scroll which you will find in the hidden drawer in your box. Once you have wrapped your mummy, seal the box with this sticker. Thieves and treasure-hunters may "lift the lid" at their peril.

Embalming the Body

Shortly after death, the internal organs were removed and the body was covered in natron, a natural salt which absorbs water. After thirty to forty days, when the body was dry, it was wiped with perfumed wine to make it smell nice and packed with sawdust to give it shape. The skin was then covered with oils to keep it from cracking, and resin, was poured over the body to preserve it.

The dark-colored resin stained the skin of mummies.

Canopic jars

Each of the removed organs were embalmed and put in containers called canopic jars. Each jar had a carved stopper which represented an Egyptian god. The canopic jars were buried with the mummy in the tomb.

From left to right, Hapy protected the lungs, Duamutef guarded the stomach, Qebehsenuef held the intestines, and Imset kept the liver.

Looking inside a mummy

Mummies can be X-rayed to give a three-dimensional image which shows both their outside surfaces and insides. By looking at X-rays of mummies, scientists can see that the ancient Egyptians also removed a mummy's brain. To do this they inserted a brain hook up the nose. The hook made a hole in the skull through which the brain could be removed. You can see the hole in this X-ray picture of an Egyptian mummy's head.

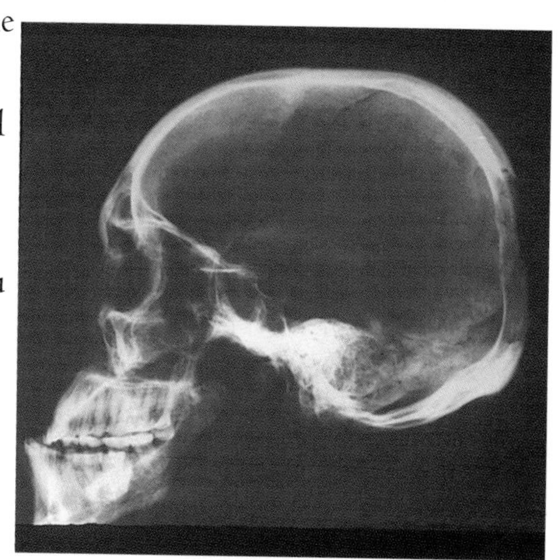

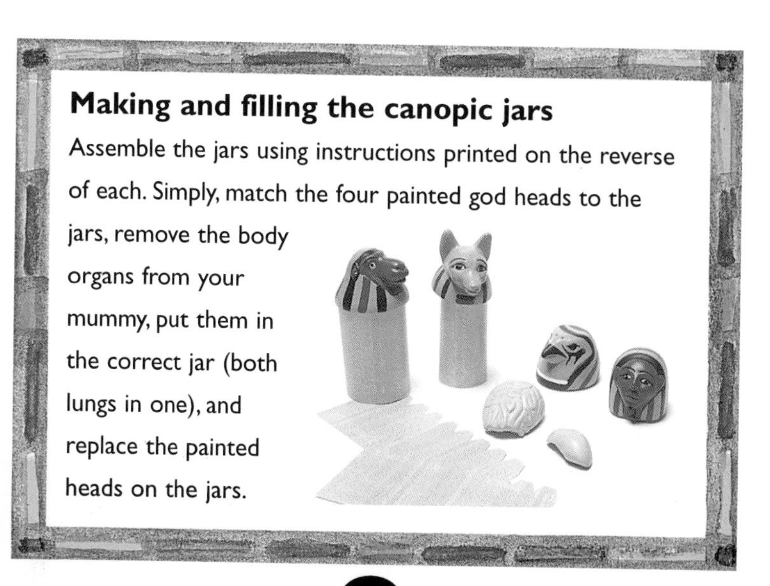

Making and filling the canopic jars

Assemble the jars using instructions printed on the reverse of each. Simply, match the four painted god heads to the jars, remove the body organs from your mummy, put them in the correct jar (both lungs in one), and replace the painted heads on the jars.

Wrapping the Body

The body was then wrapped in hundreds of feet of fine linen bandages and shrouds. Large sheets of material were placed over the body and tied in a knot at the head and feet. Sometimes fingers and toes were wrapped separately. The bandages were kept very tight to keep the mummy's shape and at the same time the linen was painted with more of the sticky resin to hold the layers together. The wrapping process took about fifteen days to complete.

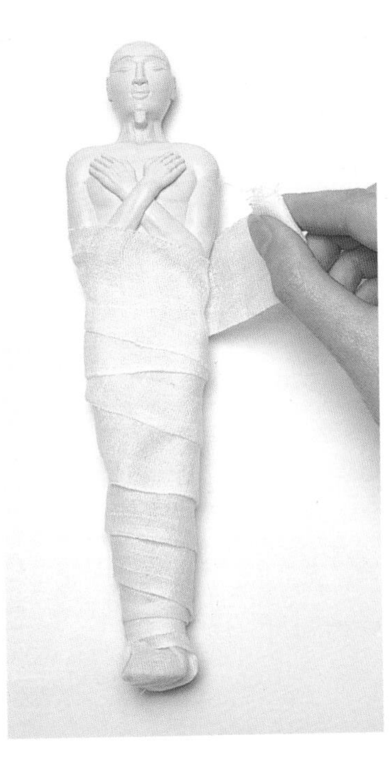

Wrapping your mummy

Once you have removed the body organs from your mummy, close the body again. Take the roll of gauze and wrap the mummy up tightly from head to toe. It is easiest if you begin by wrapping your mummy's feet, and finish by tucking the end of the bandage into one of the layers at its head.

Protective charms

The ancient Egyptians believed that a mummy needed protection in the afterlife, so they placed pieces of jewelry called amulets between the layers of bandages as the body was wrapped up. The amulets represented plants, animals, or parts of the body and warded off evil.

The eye of Horus protected the mummy's health.
The ankh was thought to bring life and strength.

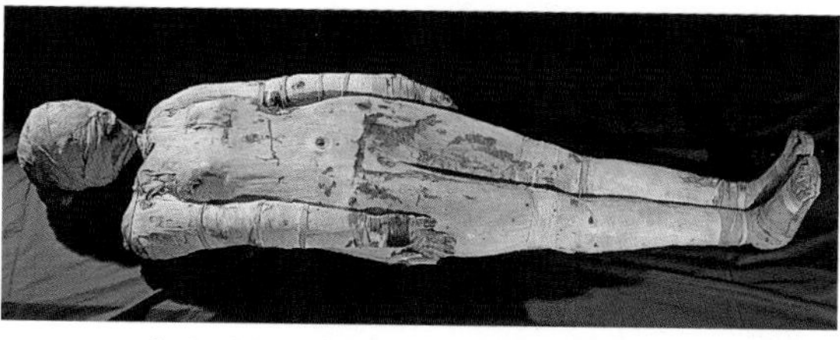

An Egyptian mummy looks like this after it has been tightly wrapped.

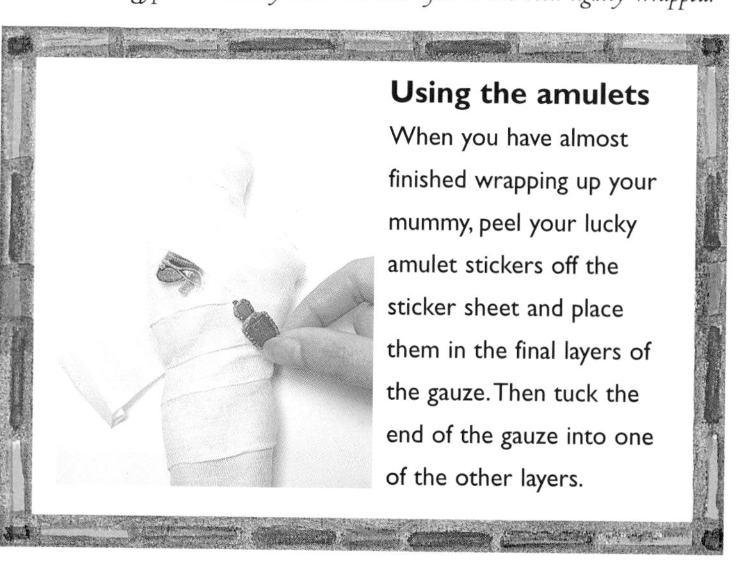

Using the amulets

When you have almost finished wrapping up your mummy, peel your lucky amulet stickers off the sticker sheet and place them in the final layers of the gauze. Then tuck the end of the gauze into one of the other layers.

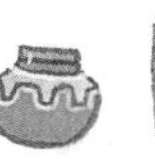

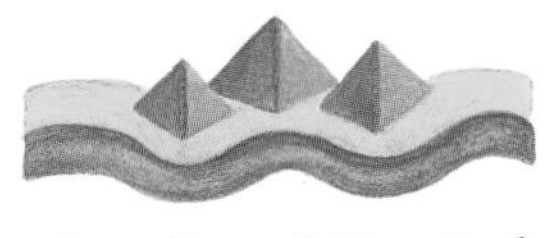

The Final Burial

After the mummy was wrapped, a funerary mask was placed over its head. It was then put into a series of three body-shaped coffins that fitted inside each other. Ancient Egyptian coffins were made out of either wood, gold, or a sort of papier-maché, called cartonnage. They were often decorated with gold foil and colored glass. Finally the coffins were then taken to a tomb or pyramid where they were stored in a large stone chest called a sarcophagus.

The funerary masks were often molded to form a portrait of the person who had died.

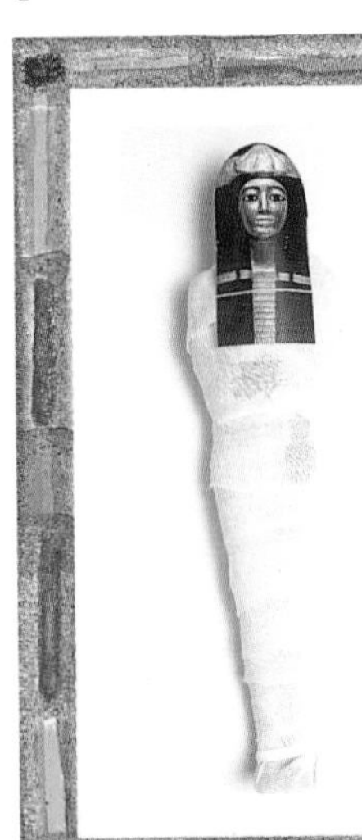

Using the mask

Place the funerary mask on the mummy's head and fasten it at the back by slotting the ends of the tabs together.

Making your own cat mummy

To assemble the cat mummy, follow the directions on the instruction sheet. The cat mummy will be a companion for your mummy in the afterlife.

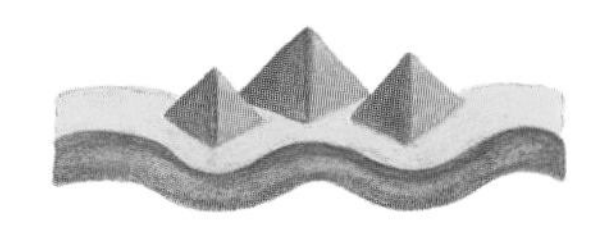

Animal mummies

As well as mummifying human bodies, the ancient Egyptians also preserved the bodies of their animals. Some animals were pets, mummified and put in their owner's tomb to join them in the afterlife. The ancient Egyptians were particularly fond of keeping cats as pets, and even had laws to protect them—if someone killed a cat, they could be punished by death! Other animals were embalmed for religious reasons because they were considered to be messengers of the gods. These spiritual mummies were buried separately in enormous animal cemeteries.

Each year, the ancient Egyptians held a national festival for the cat goddess Bastet.

Flying mummies

When archaeologists opened one of the animal cemeteries in Egypt they discovered four million embalmed ibises (birds). The ibises were dedicated to Thoth, the god of scribes and writing.

Falcons were worshipped by the ancient Egyptians. They were associated with the god Horus. This falcon, shown right, also has a funerary mask made of pure gold.

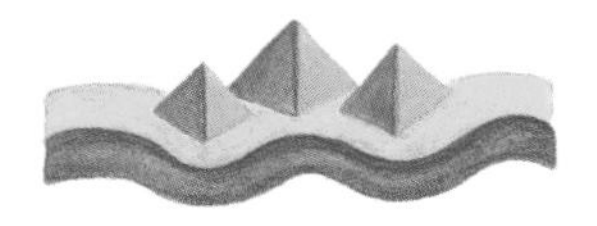

South American Mummies

The oldest mummies ever found come from Chile and Peru in South America. People there were mummifying the dead in about 3,000 B.C. Bodies were preserved by natural means, either by drying them in the hot sun, or by freezing them in the cold conditions of the Andes mountains. The mummies were placed into a crouched position, with their knees pulled up under their chin.

Some mummies from Peru were smoke-dried and rubbed with oils, resins, and herbs.

Bundled up

The South Americans wrapped their mummies inside many layers of fine cotton and wool cloth. Sometimes a false head was placed on top. False heads were made of painted cloth, stuffed with leaves.

This cross-section of a mummy bundle shows its false head and a wig of human hair hanging down the left-hand side.

Religious offerings

The Incas of Peru believed that their rulers were gods who could never die. When a ruler died, his body was mummified to keep his spirit alive. These royal mummies were worshiped as gods. The Incan people also made human sacrifices to their gods. If there was a drought or some other national crisis, the Incans sometimes killed and mummified children. The mummies were offered to the gods in the hope that conditions would improve for the rest of the people.

Shrunken heads

The Jivaro Indians were hunters who lived in the Amazon rainforests in South America. They believed that a person's soul lived inside his head. When Jivaro warriors killed an enemy, they shrunk his head to half its original size. To shrink it they first removed the brain and eyes. The head was then dried out in the hot sun. Jivaro warriors wore shrunken heads around their necks as trophies called *tsantas*.

The Javaro Indians decorated the hair of the shrunken head with beads and feathers.

Bog Mummies

Many ancient bodies, some of them over two thousand years old, have been found perfectly preserved in marshy bogs across northern Europe. It is clear that they all died violent deaths before being thrown into the bogs. As they all died in the winter it is thought that they may have been offered as sacrifices to pagan gods to make sure that spring would come again. Another idea is that they were being punished for some crime.

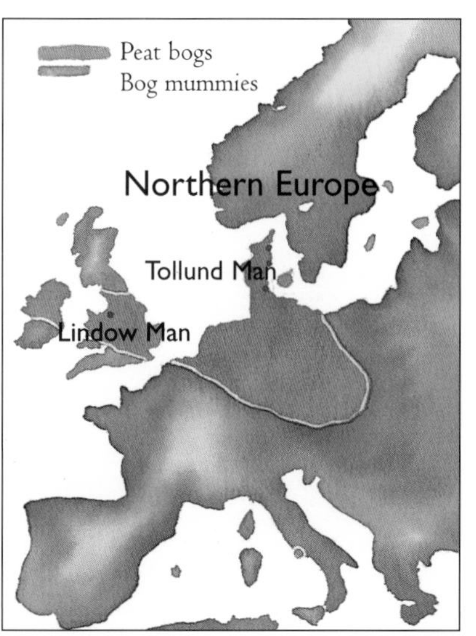

Iron Age mummies

The bog "mummies" found in northern Europe, especially in Denmark, were people who lived there as early as 500 B.C. (the Iron Age). They have all been named after the place where they were found.

Lindow Man

At 2,300 years old, Lindow Man is one of the oldest bog mummies. His body was found in a bog at Lindow Moss in the United Kingdom in 1984. Lindow Man was between twenty-five and thirty years old when he died. Scientists have found out a lot about his lifestyle from studying him—the contents of his stomach showed that his last meal was a winter cereal like porridge. They can also tell what he actually looked like.

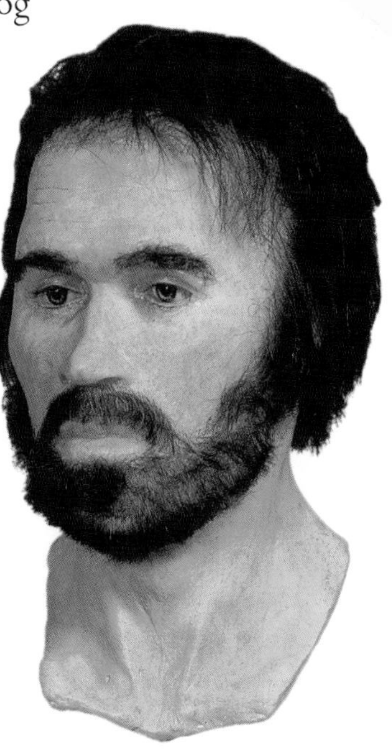

Lindow Man had dark brown hair and a full beard.

Tollund Man

In 1950 a man was found preserved in a bog at Tollund-Fen in Denmark. He had lain there for over 2000 years. Tollund Man looks as if he's asleep, but there is a noose around his neck which suggests he did not die so peacefully.

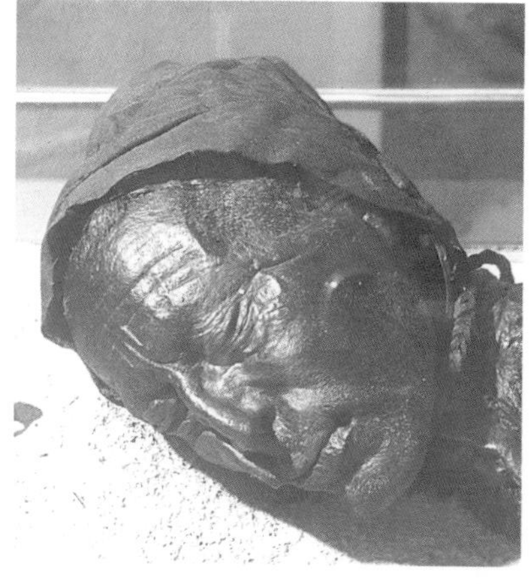

Tollund Man's face has been perfectly preserved by the acidic conditions in the bog.

Ice Mummies

On September 19, 1991, a German couple climbing in the Italian Alps, saw the top of a man's body sticking out of a glacier about 9,840 feet above in a remote mountain pass. The body had been buried under ice for over 5,000 years until warm weather melted some of the ice and uncovered him. The Iceman, as he is known, was carrying an unfinished bow, some arrows, a wooden axe with a metal head, and all the materials needed to make a fire.

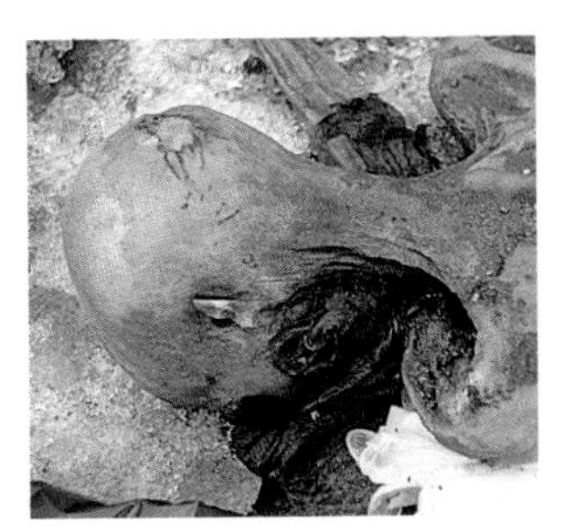

The freezing ice kept the body from rotting for many thousands of years.

Ancient mystery

No one knows why the Iceman was traveling in such bad conditions 5,300 years ago. He was about 5 feet tall, and wore patched leather clothes and shoes, and a cloak made out of grasses. Arrow wounds and head injuries were discovered on the Iceman's body, so it is possible that he was trying to escape from enemies before he got caught in a snowstorm.

Inuit burials

The burial site and frozen bodies of eight Inuit people: six women and two children, were discovered in Greenland in 1972. Their bodies had been preserved for over 500 years by freezing temperatures. These "mummies" were dressed in warm clothes and were lying on sealskin blankets in a cave with goods next to them. The Inuit people also believed that items were needed on the journey to "The Land of the Dead"— the Inuit afterlife.

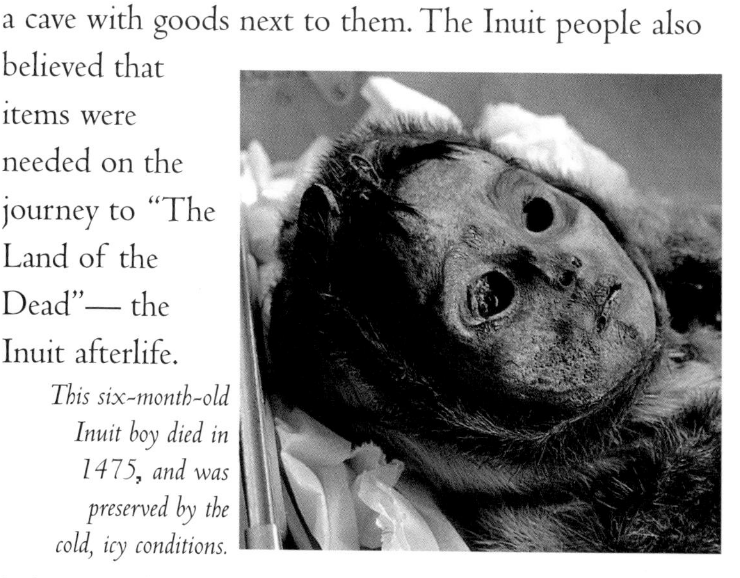

This six-month-old Inuit boy died in 1475, and was preserved by the cold, icy conditions.

The Franklin mummies

In 1845, Sir John Franklin set off from England with two ships to find a route to America via the North Pole. He was never seen again. In 1984, scientists dug up the body of John Torrington, a sailor aboard one of the ships. He had been buried in a wooden coffin on Beechey Island, inside the Arctic Circle. Frozen gravel had preserved his body almost perfectly. In 1986, the preserved bodies of two other sailors from Franklin's crew, John Hartnell and William Braine, were found.

Other Types of Mummies

A Chinese noblewoman from the Han dynasty, the Marchioness of Dai, died in about 150 B.C. She was buried in a large wooden chamber under a mound of earth, 52 feet high at Mawangdui in Changsha. The Marchioness' body had been embalmed in mercury salts, dressed in twenty layers of clothing, and buried in a nest of four beautifully painted coffins. The tomb was sealed with white clay to make it completely airtight. When the Marchioness' tomb was excavated in 1972, archaeologists found a well-preserved body.

Empty shell

Not all attempts to preserve bodies have been successful. In the 2nd century B.C., a Chinese princess, Tou Wan, was buried in a suit made of jade. The princess expected the jade to preserve her body, but she had not been embalmed. When the suit was opened, the body had rotted away.

The suit contained 2,160 pieces of jade laced together with gold wires.

Classical mummies

Egypt was conquered by the Greeks in 323 B.C. and then by the Romans in 30 B.C. Both invading cultures learned techniques of mummification from the ancient Egyptians. They embalmed the body and wrapped it in bandages, but instead of covering the mummy's head with Egyptian-style funerary masks, they put a realistic portrait over the mummy's face.

The portraits were painted on wooden panels, or sometimes modelled in plaster.

Plaster casts

In A.D. 79 the volcano Mount Vesuvius erupted and the nearby Roman town of Pompeii was covered in volcanic ash, 20 feet deep. Over 2,000 Romans were killed and the ash set around their bodies like wet cement. Over the years, the bodies decayed and the ash turned to rock, leaving perfect molds of the people. When the ruins of Pompeii were excavated, the hollow casts were filled with liquid plaster. They created perfect replicas of the dead people.

The molds were like mummies with skins of plaster.

Cryonics

Cryonics is a modern form of mummification in which people are frozen when they die. They are not preserved to travel to an afterlife, as in ancient times, but stored in the hope that in the future, scientists will cure the illnesses the patients died from and bring their bodies back to life. No one knows if cryonics works, or even if the methods used to freeze the bodies are good enough to bring people back to life. So far nobody has been taken out of storage and revived.

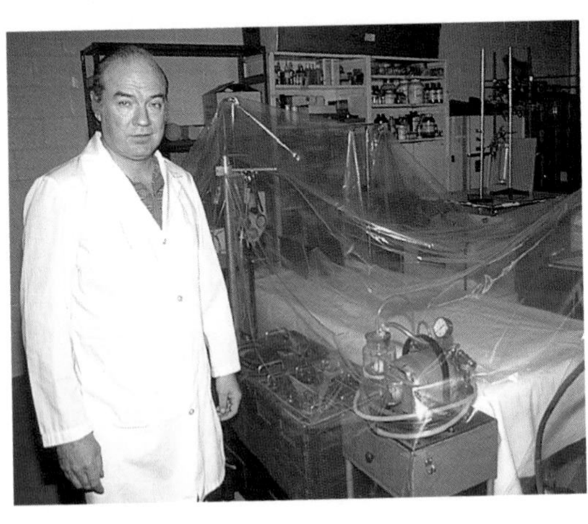

In the cryonics laboratory, doctors preserve the body by replacing the blood with a special fluid.

Still life

As soon as possible after a person dies, scientists, called cryonicists, begin to work on the body. The brain deteriorates quickly when starved of oxygen, so the cryonisists try to preserve it by supplying it with oxygen after death occurs and then freezing it in liquid nitrogen at -223.6°F.

Staying cool

The body is cooled in an ice bath, while a machine keeps the blood circulating and supplies it with oxygen. Then the blood in the body is replaced with a blood substitute, which keeps the brain supplied with oxygen. Finally the body is cooled to a temperature of -223.6°F and is stored in a metal cylinder of liquid nitrogen.

People can be stored in liquid nitrogen for many years. Hopefully, in the future, a cure will be found for their illness.

Uncertain future

People who want to take a chance that their bodies might be brought back to life, can sign up with a cryonics organization, which will plan to freeze and store them when they die. People can choose to have their entire bodies frozen—or just their heads or brains in the hope that they might be given new bodies. These people are willing to pay a lot of money to have their bodies preserved, even though there is no proof that cryonics works. Some people have already been stored for thirty years. Perhaps one day they will live in a very different world from the one they had known.

Index